BRAVE
like a
GIRL ! x

Published 2020 by Lerrags Clan Publishing

Printed in the United States of America by Author2Market

Book Designed by Electronic Ink

Book Formatting and book cover provided by Trisha Fuentes

ISBN 978-1-7346534-9-6

DEDICATED TO:

all the <u>brave</u>
boys and girls in
the world!

Hi! My name is ANDY. Recently,
my teacher Mr. Carmichael (we call him Mr.C for short)
gave my class an assignment.

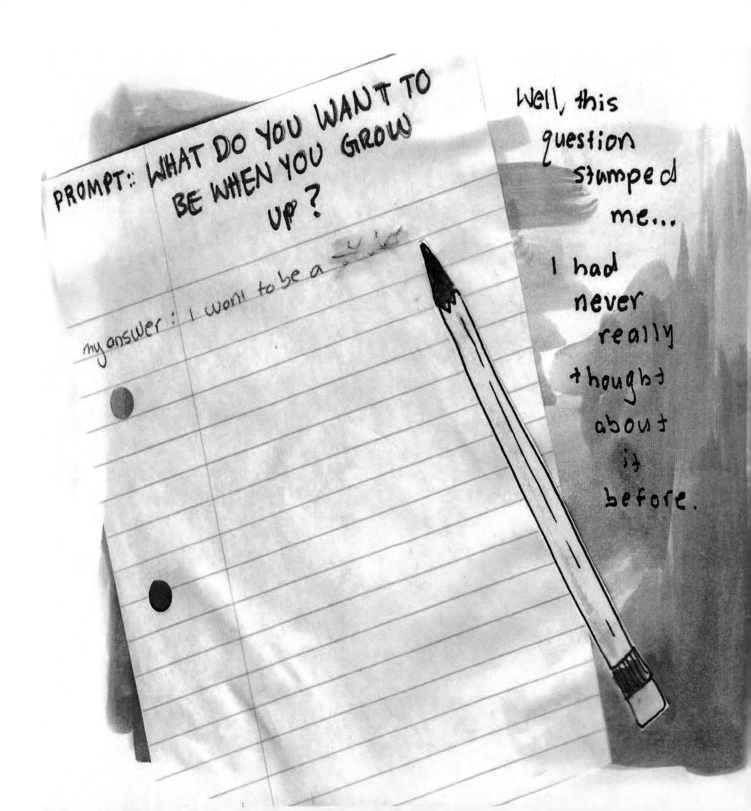

MARIE CURIE
french-polish physicist
(1867 - 1934)

This is Marie Curie! She was a scientist! She believed all people should be educated. Marie went to college and become an incredible scientist. In fact she discovered two chemical elements — Radium and Polonium.
Did she do science experiments, like we do in class?
Yes! Even when things went wrong, she persisted (a fancy word for kept trying).
FUN FACT: the notebooks she wrote in are still radioactive.

AMELIA EARHART
american aviator
(1897 - 1939)

Meet AMELIA EARHART. She was the first woman to fly solo across the Atlantic ocean! She went on her first airplane ride in 1920. From then on she kept going with her passion of aviation (a fancy word for flying planes). Some people told her she wouldn't be able to do it, but she didn't let that stop her!
Amazing! She was so brave to fly across the ocean alone. I could fly in the sky just like her someday!

FRIDA KAHLO
mexican artist
(1907-1954)

This is Frida! She was a painter from Mexico. She is best known for her amazing self portraits that deal with themes of identity, humans, and even hard topics like death. She was in an accident as a young girl, but kept pursuing her dream of being an artist! Sometimes that meant she had to paint from her hospital bed!
It can be scary showing people who you are, but she was so brave to express herself through art!
Maybe I should try painting a self portrait!

"ROSIE the RIVETER"
icon/symbol
of WW II
(1943-1945)

"Rosie the Riveter" is a famous fictional Character of World war 2. She was used by the American government in a campaign urging women to join the workforce!

Women began working in factories as engineers! They made munitions, built ships and constructed airplanes.

FUN FACT: the campaign coined the phrase "we can do it!"

ROSA PARKS
american activist
(1913 - 2005)

Meet Rosa! she grew up in a time where some people were discriminated (a fancy word for left out) based on their skin color. Rosa knew this was wrong and wanted everyone to have equal rights. she made it her job to be an activist for the rights of African Americans!
Wow! she must have been very brave! I want to help everyone feel loved and equal!
EQUALITY

KATHERINE JOHNSON
american mathmatician
(1918 – present)

This is katherine Johnson, she was a computer for NASA!
A computer?
Yes, but not like the machine; she computed (a fancy word for calculated) numbers that helped John Glenn get to space. He was the first person to orbit (a fancy word for go around) the Earth, thanks to katherine!
Neat! That sounds like an important job. I want to learn math like her!

MALALA YOUSAF'ZAI
pakistani activist
(1997 – present)

This is Malala. She is from a country called Pakistan; she is an education activist. She stands up for girls rights to go to school! Some people in the world dont get to have an education, and she wants that to change!
Oh! Everyone deserves to learn! I want to be brave and stand up for other kids like me.
NOW IT'S TIME TO HEAD BACK TO CLASS

WOW! I never knew how many wonderful things I could do and be when I grow up. There are so many inspiring people in the world.

I COULD BE A...

Pilot like AMELIA!

Mathmatician like KATHERINE!

Scientist like MARIE!

Artist like FRIDA!

Activist like ROSA!

teacher like MALALA (or mr. C.!)!

Engineer like the FACTORY GIRLS!

I can do anything, and so can YOU. I think I finally know how to answer Mr. C's question...

PROMPT: WHAT DO YOU WANT TO
BE WHEN YOU GROW
UP?

my answer : I want to be

BRAVE!
x

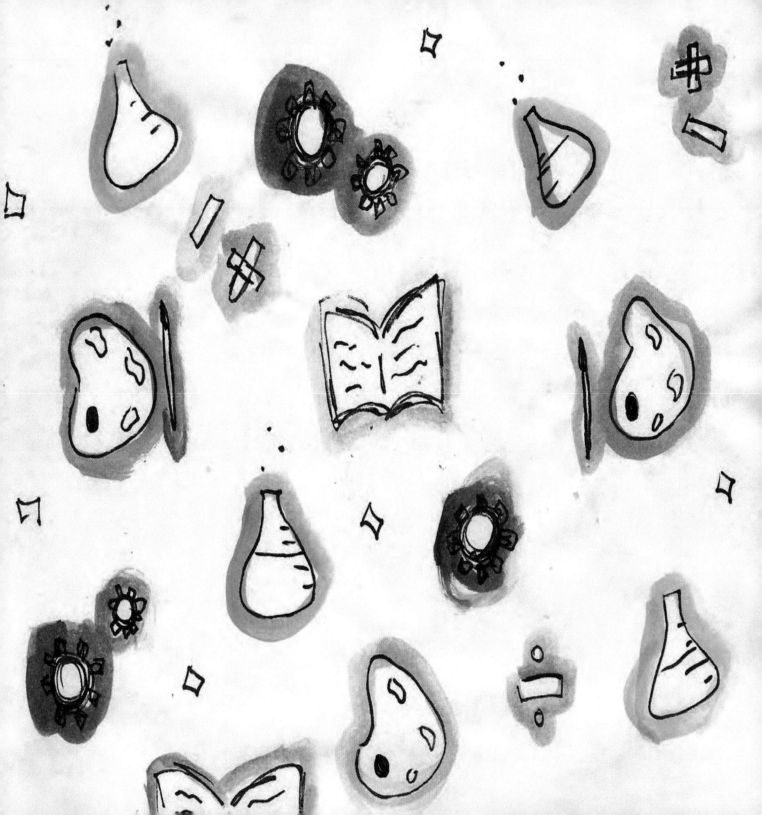

Made in the USA
Las Vegas, NV
26 February 2022

44617010R00019